About the Author: Dr. Jada Jackson, LMHC, LPC-S

Dr. Jada Jackson is a Licensed Mental Health Cou.. Professional Counselor-Supervisor (LPC-S) with over two decades of experience in the fields of mental health and counseling. As a seasoned therapist, Dr. Jackson is deeply committed to helping individuals, couples, and families navigate life's challenges by equipping them with practical tools to manage stress, overcome trauma, and foster emotional well-being.

Dr. Jackson holds advanced degrees in Counselor Education and Supervision, and Human Services Counseling, solidifying her expertise in the realms of trauma therapy, cognitive behavioral therapy (CBT), and emotional wellness. She has built a reputation for her work with athletes, high-performance individuals, and professional clients, helping them to optimize their mental and emotional health.

Beyond her clinical practice, Dr. Jackson is a sought-after speaker, educator, and media personality, regularly appearing as a mental health expert on national television and news outlets. She has also been an influential advocate for mental health awareness and diversity in media, using her platform to inspire change and promote healing through education and advocacy.

As a compassionate supervisor and mentor, Dr. Jackson provides guidance to emerging mental health professionals, focusing on building ethical, effective counseling practices. Her holistic approach to therapy incorporates both psychological and spiritual perspectives, empowering clients to achieve lasting transformation.

With *The Therapy Toolbox Works*, Dr. Jackson combines her wealth of experience and knowledge to create a resource that is both accessible and empowering for therapists and clients alike. Her dedication to improving mental health outcomes continues to inspire individuals to take control of their well-being and live life to its fullest potential.

Dr. Jackson resides in Dallas, where she continues to teach, supervise, and support those seeking emotional freedom and mental clarity.

TABLE
OF CONTENTS

TABLE
OF CONTENTS

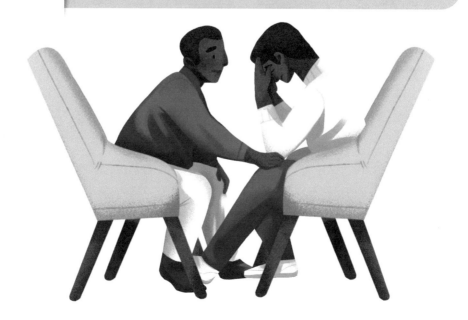

Introduction

Purpose of the Book

In today's fast-paced world, mental health professionals are constantly navigating the complexities of both patients' needs and their personal development as practitioners. *The Therapy Toolbox Works: Empowering Therapists & Patients* aims to serve as a comprehensive guide for therapists who want to expand their practical skills while fostering deep therapeutic relationships with their clients. The book bridges evidence-based techniques with real-world practice, offering tools that can be applied across diverse clinical settings. Whether you're a seasoned clinician or a new therapist, the purpose of this book is to empower both you and your clients to achieve lasting change and growth.

How to Use This Book

This book is designed as a hands-on resource, complete with practical exercises, client worksheets, and step-by-step interventions. Each chapter provides insight into common challenges therapists face, offering effective techniques to address those challenges in a therapeutic setting. You'll find various "tools" organized by theme and issue, allowing you to quickly access the right strategy for your client's specific needs. Whether you choose to read through it cover to cover or skip directly to the tools that are most relevant to you, the book is structured for flexibility and ease of use.

HOW THE BRAIN WORKS

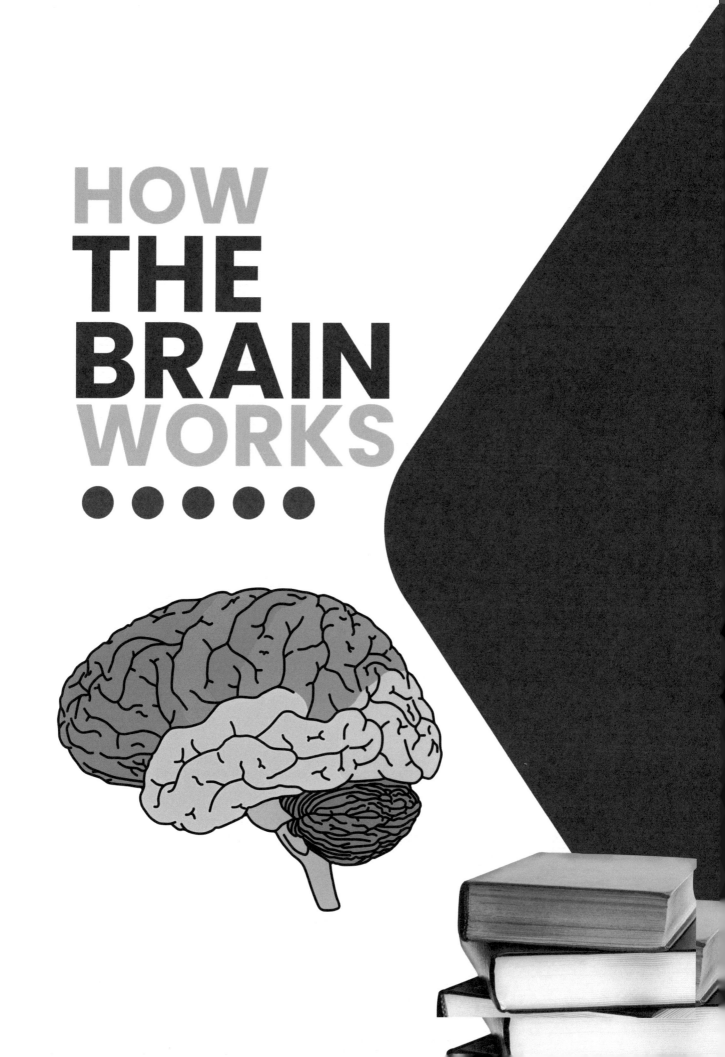

How the Brain Works with
Emotion

The brain plays a crucial role in processing and experiencing emotions. Emotions are complex psychological and physiological responses to external stimuli that can influence our behavior, thoughts, and physical sensations. The brain works with emotion through several interconnected structures. Ident

@DrJadaJackson

prefrontal cortex

The right lobe is linked to negative emotions, such as fear, aggression, and sadness, while the left lobe helps to regulate negative emotions and put them in check.

thalamus

Responsible for relaying sensory and motor signals to the cerebral cortex and also plays a role in the regulation of consciousness, sleep, and alertness.

neocortex

Responsible for higher cognitive functions, such as language and consciousness, and also plays a role in emotional processing.

hypothalamus

The key that turns our emotions into physical responses.

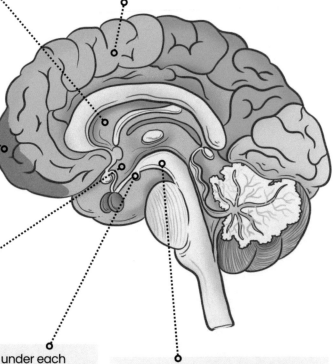

An almond-shaped structure located under each hemisphere of the brain and is responsible for regulating emotion and memory, including those associated with the brain's reward system, stress, and the "fight or flight" response when someone perceives a threat.

amygdala

Plays an important role in memory formation, learning, and spatial navigation. It provides context for emotional meaning.

hippocampus

The Stress Response
Fight - Flight - Freeze

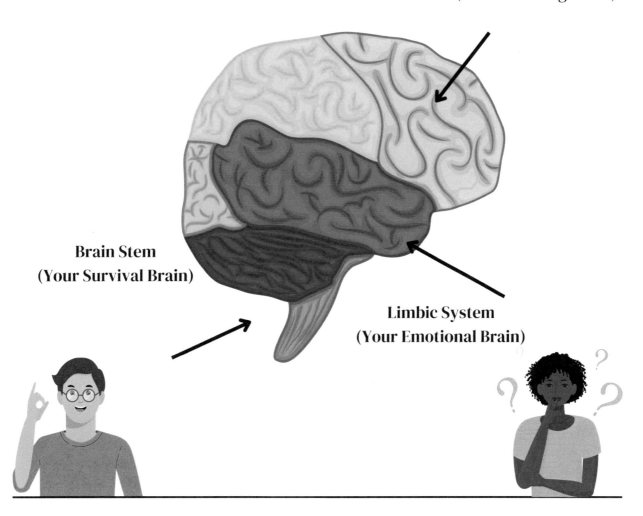

Frontal Lobe
(Your Thinking Brain)

Brain Stem
(Your Survival Brain)

Limbic System
(Your Emotional Brain)

- **Survival - Brain Stem:** Responsible for basic, life-sustaining functions like breathing, heart rate, and blood pressure, which operate automatically and without conscious thought.
- **Emotional - Limbic System:** Processes emotions, forms emotional memories, and influences motivation and behavior.
- **Thinking - Frontal Lobe:** Manages higher cognitive processes, including problem-solving, reasoning, planning, and decision-making.

Fight, Flight, Freeze, Fawn

Your fight response

The fight response is triggered when a person perceives a threat and reacts with aggression or confrontation. It prepares the body to defend itself, leading to increased adrenaline, heart rate, and muscle tension. This response can manifest as anger, frustration, or attempts to control or overpower the perceived danger.

Your flight response

The flight response occurs when a person senses danger and instinctively wants to escape. It involves fleeing from the threat, physically or emotionally. The body prepares by increasing heart rate and alertness, allowing quick decision-making. This response is driven by fear, avoidance, or the urge to run away from danger.

Your freeze response

The freeze response occurs when a person feels immobilized in the face of a threat, unable to act or make decisions. They may feel numb, with a blank mind, often due to feeling overwhelmed or powerless.

Your fawn response

The fawn response involves seeking to appease others to avoid conflict or harm. Individuals prioritize others' needs over their own, often due to fear of rejection or confrontation, leading to people-pleasing and neglect of personal boundaries.

@DrJadaJackson

HOW
THOUGHT
TRAPS
WORKS
● ● ● ● ●

Thought Traps

Over time, we all fall into patterns of thinking that don't always serve us well. You may recognize some of these unhelpful thought habits more than others—maybe they even sound a little too familiar. The good news? Once you spot these thinking traps, you can start catching them in real time, especially when you're feeling overwhelmed or distressed. And when you notice them, you create space to step back, challenge them, and see things from a clearer, more helpful perspective. It's about taking back control and finding a way through the noise of negative thinking.

@DrJadaJackson

Labeling

Assigning global, negative labels to yourself or others based on specific behaviors. For example, "I'm a loser" or "They're a bad person."

Catastrophizing

Expecting the worst possible outcome in any situation. For example, "If I make a mistake at work, I'll get fired and never find another job."

Blaming

Holding others responsible for your emotional state, instead of recognizing your own role in managing your emotions. For example, "I'm angry because you made me angry."

Should Statements

Imposing rigid expectations on yourself or others, leading to guilt or frustration when they're not met. For example, "I should always be on time."

Emotional Reasoning

Believing that negative emotions reflect reality. For example, "I feel worthless, so I must be worthless."

Personalization

Blaming yourself for events outside of your control, or taking responsibility for things that are not your fault. For example, "It's my fault they're upset."

Discounting the Positive

Dismissing positive experiences or achievements by insisting they don't count. For example, "I did well, but anyone could have done that."

Magnification or Minimization

Exaggerating the importance of negative events (magnification) or downplaying the significance of positive events (minimization). For example, "My mistake was huge" or "My success doesn't really matter."

Mind Reading

Assuming you know what others are thinking without any evidence. For example, "They didn't say hello, so they must not like me."

Fortune Telling

Predicting negative outcomes without any factual basis. For example, "I know I'll fail the exam."

Overgeneralization

Making broad generalizations based on a single event or a small amount of evidence. For example, "I didn't get the job; I'll never get a job."

Mental Filter

Focusing only on the negative aspects of a situation and ignoring the positives. For example, "I made a mistake during the presentation; the whole thing was a disaster.

Challenging Thought Traps

Reframing your unhelpful thoughts renews your perspective

@DrJadaJackson

Identify
Identify the Distorted Thought: Recognize negative thought patterns

Examine
Examine the Evidence: Evaluate facts supporting or contradicting the thought.

Reframe
Reframe the Thought: Replace it with a balanced perspective.

Assess
Assess the Impact: Consider how the thought affects you.

Practice
Practice and Repeat: Consistently apply these steps to develop healthier thinking.

1   **2**   **3**   **4**   **5**

1 — Name Your Feelings: Are you sad, anxious, angry? Rate Intensity: On a scale of 1-10, how strong is the emotion?

2 — Write Down the Thought: Start by clearly writing out the negative thought you're experiencing. What evidence supports this thought? What evidence contradicts this thought? Under each question, list specific facts, events, or experiences that either support or contradict the thought.

3 — When you notice a negative thought, consciously rephrase it into a balanced statement by considering both the positives and negatives to achieve a more realistic perspective.

Example of Reframing a Negative Thought:
- Negative Thought: "I'm terrible at public speaking; I completely ruined that presentation."
- Reframed Thought: "The presentation didn't go as smoothly as I wanted, but I've done well in past speaking engagements. I can identify areas to improve and do better next time."

4 — Take a moment to reflect on how the thought influences your feelings and actions, noting whether it leads to positive or negative outcomes in your life.

5 — Name Your Feelings: Are you sad, anxious, angry? Rate Intensity: On a scale of 1-10, how strong is the emotion?

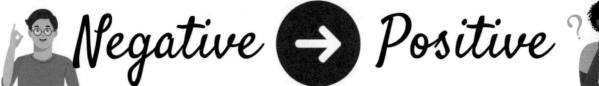# Negative → Positive

Reframe negative thoughts by recognizing them, questioning their validity, and consciously replacing them with more positive and realistic perspectives.

My negative thought: _____
_____
_____
_____

Evidence for my thought:
_____
_____
_____
_____
_____
_____
_____

Evidence against my thought:
_____
_____
_____
_____
_____
_____
_____

How can I reframe my negative thought to a more realistic one?
_____
_____
_____
_____
_____

Everyday Trauma: Understanding Its Impact and Healing

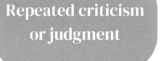

Repeated criticism or judgment

Constant stress at work or home

Being ignored or feeling unimportant

Difficult breakups or friendship conflicts

Witnessing harm to others (even in media)

Financial difficulties or job loss

Here are some signs that everyday experiences may be affecting you deeply:

Emotional Symptoms: Feeling overwhelmed, anxious, or sad more than usual.
Physical Symptoms: Headaches, stomach problems, fatigue, or muscle tension.
Behavioral Symptoms: Difficulty concentrating, avoiding certain people or places, or using unhealthy coping mechanisms like overeating or withdrawing from others.
Relational Symptoms: Trouble communicating, feeling disconnected from loved ones, or experiencing conflict more often.

@DrJadaJackson

SETTING
HEALTHY
BOUNDARIES
FOR LIFE

Essential Questions for Setting Healthy Boundaries in Every Area of Life

 Emotional Boundaries
- How do I feel when others share their problems with me? Do I feel drained or overwhelmed?
- Am I comfortable expressing my feelings to others? Do I feel heard and respected?
- How do I protect my emotions when someone is upset or angry around me?
- Do I often take on other people's feelings as my own? How can I avoid this?

 Physical Boundaries
- What personal space or physical touch am I comfortable with in different settings (work, family, friends)?
- How do I react when someone invades my personal space? How can I communicate my need for space?
- Are there activities or situations where I feel physically unsafe? How can I avoid or protect myself in these situations?

 Time Boundaries
- How do I feel when others ask for my time or energy? Do I often say "yes" when I want to say "no"?
- Do I schedule enough personal time for rest, hobbies, or relaxation?
- How can I be more assertive in protecting my time for self-care and important priorities?
- What boundaries can I set to prevent work or other obligations from overtaking my free time?

 Friendship Boundaries:
- Am I fostering healthy friendships where mutual respect and boundaries are upheld?
- Do I feel comfortable communicating my needs and limits in my friendships?
- Am I able to maintain my sense of self and independence within my friendships?

 Mental Boundaries
- Am I comfortable with others challenging my opinions, beliefs, or ideas?
- Do I feel pressured to agree with others, even when I disagree? How can I stay true to my own values?
- How do I handle criticism or advice from others? Do I allow it to affect my self-worth?
- How can I protect my mental space from negativity or unhealthy influences?

Essential Questions for Setting Healthy Boundaries in Every Area of Life

 Work Boundaries
- Do I feel overwhelmed by my workload or the demands of others at work? How can I manage this?
- How comfortable am I saying "no" to additional tasks or projects when I am already busy?
- Do I regularly take breaks and protect my personal time from work-related interruptions?
- How do I maintain professionalism while also protecting my personal needs?

 Digital Boundaries
- How much time am I spending online or on social media? Does it impact my mental health or relationships?
- Am I comfortable with how much access others have to me via phone, text, or social media?
- How do I feel when I see certain content online? Should I unfollow or mute accounts that cause stress or negativity?
- How can I limit my digital time to stay present and mindful in my everyday life?

 Financial Boundaries
- Am I comfortable with how I manage my finances, and do I set limits on spending or lending money to others?
- How do I feel when friends or family ask for financial help? Am I able to say "no" if needed?
- Am I saving and spending in a way that aligns with my financial goals?
- What financial boundaries can I set to protect my personal and family's needs?

 Intimacy Boundaries
- What level of emotional and physical intimacy am I comfortable with in my relationships?
- Do I feel safe and respected when discussing or engaging in intimate activities?
- How do I communicate my needs, limits, and consent in intimate situations?
- Am I comfortable with how my partner or others respond to my boundaries around intimacy?
- What steps can I take to ensure my emotional and physical safety in intimate relationships?

HEALTHY BOUNDARIES: QUICK GUIDE

Boundaries are personal limits we set to protect our physical, emotional, mental, and relational well-being. They help define what is acceptable behavior from others and what is not, ensuring we maintain a healthy sense of self and respectful interactions in different areas of life. Boundaries can vary from physical space to emotional needs, helping manage time, energy, and resources effectively.

PHYSICAL BOUNDARIES

Physical Boundaries: Protecting personal space, touch preferences, and physical well-being. Example: "I prefer not to be hugged."

EMOTIONAL BOUNDARIES

Guarding emotional energy and managing how others affect your feelings. Example: "I need space to process my emotions without advice."

MENTAL BOUNDARIES

Mental Boundaries: Respecting opinions, thoughts, and beliefs. Example: "I respect that we have different viewpoints, but I don't want to argue."

TIME BOUNDARIES

Time Boundaries: Prioritizing your time and commitments. Example: "I can only stay for an hour."

RELATIONSHIP BOUNDARIES

Relationship Boundaries: Establishing expectations for intimate, family, and friendship relationships. Example: "I need honesty and trust in our relationship."

MATERIAL BOUNDARIES

Material Boundaries: Managing how your possessions and resources are used by others. Example: "I'm not comfortable lending out my car."

SPIRITUAL BOUNDARIES

Spiritual Boundaries: Protecting beliefs and practices from being disrespected or imposed upon. Example: "I need time for personal prayer and reflection."

SEXUAL BOUNDARIES

Sexual Boundaries: Setting limits around sexual touch, consent, and activity. Example: "I'm not comfortable with that level of intimacy."

@DrJadaJackson

@DrJadaJackson

SETTING
SMART
GOALS
FOR LIFE

SMART Goals Worksheet

Objective: Use the SMART framework to create actionable, realistic goals. SMART stands for Specific, Measurable, Achievable, Relevant, and Time-bound.

➡ Step 1: Set Your SMART Goal

Specific - What exactly do you want to achieve?
Example: "I want to walk 30 minutes every morning before work."

Your Specific Goal:

_____

Measurable - How will you track progress?*
Example: "I'll use a fitness app to track my steps daily."

Your Measure:

_____

Achievable - Is this goal realistic for you?
Example: "I have walking shoes and live in a safe neighborhood."

Is it achievable? (Yes/No) Why?

_____

Relevant - Why is this goal important to you?
Example: "I want to improve my health and energy."

Why is it important?

_____

Time-bound - What's your deadline for this goal?
Example: "I want to walk every day for the next 3 months."

Your Deadline:

_____

SMART Goals Worksheet cont.

 Step 2: Plan for Obstacles

What challenges might come up? How will you overcome them?
Example: "If I feel too tired, I'll set out my clothes the night before."

Your Obstacles & Solutions:

_____

 Step 3: Accountability

Who can you share your goal with for support?
Example: "I'll check in with a friend weekly."

Your Support System:

_____

 Step 4: Progress Check-In

When will you check in on your progress?
Example: "I'll review my progress weekly."

Check-In Date:

_____

 Step 5: Success Reflection

Did you achieve your goal? How do you feel?
Example: "I walked daily for 3 months and feel healthier!"

Your Reflection:

_____

SMART Goal Summary:

By setting a specific, measurable, achievable, relevant, and time-bound goal,
you'll increase your chances of success.

EMBRACING
EMOTIONAL
REGULATION
FOR LIFE

Emotion Identification and Regulation Worksheet

Objective:

This worksheet helps clients recognize, understand, and regulate their emotions. By identifying emotional triggers and bodily sensations, clients can develop healthier ways of managing their emotional responses.

Step 1: Emotion Identification

Recognize the Situation
Describe a recent situation where you felt a strong emotion.
Example: "I had an argument with my friend about being late to meet me."

Situation:

_____

Identify Your Emotion
What emotion did you experience in this situation?
Refer to the list below to help identify your emotion.
- Common Emotions: Angry, Sad, Anxious, Overwhelmed, Excited, Fearful, Frustrated, Embarrassed, Joyful, Lonely, Guilty, Grateful.

Your Emotion:

_____

Step 2: Understanding Triggers and Body Sensations

What Triggered the Emotion?
What specific event or thought led to this emotion?
Example: "My friend's comment about me overreacting triggered my anger."

Trigger:

_____

Physical Sensations
What physical sensations did you notice in your body?
Some examples include tense muscles, rapid heartbeat, clenched fists, headaches, etc.

Physical Sensations:

_____

Emotion Identification and Regulation Worksheet cont.

Step 3: Emotional Reaction

Behavioral Response How did you react in this situation? What did you do or say?
Example: "I yelled at my friend and stormed out."

Your Reaction:

_____

Reflection on the Reaction Was this reaction helpful or unhelpful? How did it affect you and others involved?
Example: "It made the situation worse because I hurt my friend's feelings."

Reflection:

_____

Step 4: Emotional Regulation Techniques

Regulation Strategies What techniques could you have used to regulate your emotion?
Some common emotional regulation strategies include:
Deep Breathing
Counting to Ten
Mindfulness
Grounding Techniques (e.g., focusing on your senses)
Self-Talk (e.g., "I am capable of handling this calmly.")
Physical Exercise

Which Techniques Could You Use?

_____

Try the Strategy: Practice one regulation strategy next time you feel this emotion.
Record your experience here.

Strategy Tried:

_____

Outcome:

_____

WINDOW OF TOLERANCE

The Window of Tolerance is like your personal comfort zone for handling life's ups and downs.

@DrJadaJackson

HYPERAROUSAL

- Experiencing intense anxiety that may lead to panic attacks.
- Feeling overwhelmed and out of control.
- Urge to fight or run away.

DYSREGULATION

- Feelings of frustration and agitation intensify.
- Uncomfortable emotions are increasing, but you remain in control.
- You may become easily irritated or impatient.

WINDOW OF TOLERANCE

When you're within this "window," you feel balanced and can manage stress, emotions, and everyday challenges effectively. You're alert but calm, able to think clearly, and respond to situations appropriately.

- Feeling stressed
- Upsetting memories.
- Feeling anxious or worried.
- Experiencing rejection
- Feeling abandoned or lonely

Stressors that decrease your tolerance

Skills that increase your tolerance

- Cognitive reframing
- Mindfulness
- Guided imagery
- Meditation
- Grounding
- Positive self talk
- Deep breathing

DYSREGULATION

- Uncomfortable feelings are starting to increase.
- Frustration and agitation are intensifying.
- Approaching the point of shutting down, but still in control.

HYPERAROUSAL

- Experiencing physical numbness and a sense of being frozen.
- Feeling disconnected and mentally zoned out.
- Lacking energy and feeling lethargic.

Types of Triggers: Everyday Responses
@DrJadaJackson

 ## Emotional Triggers

Feelings of sadness, anger, or anxiety from a past experience (e.g., rejection, abandonment).

Example: Receiving critical feedback from a colleague or friend.

 ## Relationship Triggers

Conflict, criticism, or negative interactions with loved ones that can evoke strong emotional responses.

Example: A partner forgets an anniversary or an important date.

 ## Environmental Triggers

Specific places or situations (e.g., a particular room, city, or type of setting) that remind someone of. trauma or distress.

Example: Walking into a room where a past argument occurred.

 ## Social Triggers

Social interactions or group dynamics, such as feeling left out, judged, or overwhelmed in crowds.

Example: Being excluded from a social gathering or group chat.

 ## Sensory Triggers

Specific smells, sounds, tastes, or sights that bring back memories of past experiences (e.g., perfume reminding someone of an ex-partner).

Example: Smelling a perfume that a past partner used to wear.

 ## Physical Triggers

Changes in physical condition (e.g., lack of sleep, hunger, or illness) that can influence mood or emotions.

Example: Experiencing lack of sleep due to a busy schedule.

 ## Thought Triggers

Intrusive or negative thoughts, including cognitive distortions that lead to spirals of anxiety or depression.

Example: Thinking "I'm not good enough" when comparing oneself to a more successful peer.

 ## Work/School Triggers

Stressors related to job demands, deadlines, or academic pressure.

Example: Receiving an urgent email from a boss late at night.

 ## Media Triggers

Content in TV shows, movies, social media, or news that elicits a strong emotional reaction, often related to violence, trauma, or upsetting events.

Example: Seeing news coverage of a tragic event (e.g., a natural disaster or violent incident).

 ## Financial Triggers

Worries or conflicts about money, bills, or financial instability.

Example: Receiving an unexpected bill or notice of a financial obligation.

Events, experiences, or thoughts that provoke deep questioning about one's beliefs, purpose, or the meaning of life.

Example: Having a crisis of faith or encountering someone with opposing religious beliefs.

 ## Grief Triggers

Stimuli—such as people, places, objects, or dates—that remind an individual of a loss, typically the death of a loved one or another significant personal loss.

Example: Seeing a birthday reminder or a picture of a loved one who has passed away.

Coping with Triggers: Techniques for Mental Strength

Identify your trigger: **Identify your coping skill:**

Trigger Thermometer

@DrJadaJackson

A Trigger Thermometer is a tool to help you recognize the intensity of your emotional or psychological response to various triggers. It allows you to gauge you emotional state and take action before the reaction escalates.

Low/Green (Calm)
- Description: You feel in control, calm, and able to handle any challenges. No significant emotional reaction to potential triggers.
- Examples: Relaxed, content, or slightly aware of potential stress but unaffected.
- Action: Continue practicing self-care and mindfulness. No intervention needed.

Mild/Green (Aware)
- Description: You're beginning to notice discomfort or slight tension but are still able to manage it effectively. You are aware of the trigger but can easily redirect your focus.
- Examples: Feeling slightly anxious, irritated, or distracted.
- Action: Take a few deep breaths, ground yourself, or step away to reset before emotions escalate.

Moderate/Yellow (Distressed)
- Description: Emotions are starting to intensify. You feel uneasy, anxious, or upset and may have difficulty concentrating or staying calm.
- Examples: Irritability, racing thoughts, rapid heartbeat, or feeling overwhelmed by the trigger.
- Action: Use coping strategies, such as deep breathing, reframing thoughts, or removing yourself from the triggering environment.

High/Orange (Upset)
- Description: Strong emotional reaction. You may feel overwhelmed, anxious, angry, or fearful. It becomes difficult to control your response, and you're close to reacting impulsively.
- Examples: Yelling, crying, pacing, or feeling like you're losing control.
- Action: Take immediate steps to calm down —use a timeout, deep breathing, meditation, or reach out for support.

Critical Red (Crisis)
- Description: Intense emotional reaction. You are no longer in control of your emotions and may react in ways that are unhealthy or harmful. You feel panic, rage, or complete overwhelm.
- Examples: Shouting, physical reactions (punching walls, pacing), or feeling like you can't cope.
- Action: Remove yourself from the situation, seek immediate support, or engage in emergency coping strategies like calling a therapist, friend, or crisis hotline.

Anger Management Worksheet
Step-by-Step Guide for Managing Anger

This worksheet is designed to help individuals identify, understand, and manage their anger effectively. Use it during therapy sessions to guide clients through a structured approach to handling anger in healthy and productive ways.

Identify Your Triggers

Understanding what sets off your anger is the first step in managing it. Write down situations, people, or events that commonly trigger your anger. List 3-5 common triggers that cause you to feel angry.

Recognize the Signs of Anger

Anger often shows up physically and emotionally. Identifying these signs early can help you respond before the anger escalates. Write down the physical and emotional signs you experience when you're getting angry.

Rate Your Anger

Use a scale of 1-10 to rate your anger levels. This will help you gauge how intense your anger is in different situations. Recall a recent incident that made you angry and rate your anger on a scale from 1-10.

Pause and Breathe

Practice deep breathing: Inhale slowly for 4 counts, hold for 4 counts, and exhale for 6 counts. Repeat this process for at least 2 minutes when you notice anger building. This is called the "cool-down technique."

Challenge Your Thoughts

Anger often stems from irrational thoughts or cognitive distortions. Learning to reframe these thoughts can reduce your anger. Write down the negative thoughts you have when you're angry, then challenge them with a more rational perspective.

Choose a Constructive Response

Instead of reacting impulsively, choose how you'll respond to the situation. It's important to express anger in a healthy way without hurting yourself or others. Write down how you could respond to the situation constructively.

Practice Self-Soothing Techniques

Learning to calm yourself in the moment is crucial. List 3 self-soothing techniques that help you calm down when you're angry. Examples: Taking a 10-minute walk. Listening to calming music. Journaling about how I feel.

@DrJadaJackson

Messages from Your Emotions @DrJadaJackson

Negative emotions are a natural part of the human experience, and they serve as signals or messages that provide valuable information about our inner state, our needs, and our reactions to various situations. Here's a list of some common negative emotions and what they may say to us:

Anger:
Message: "Your boundaries have been violated or your needs are not being met. Take action to address the issue."

Sadness:
Message: "You have experienced a loss or disappointment. It's okay to grieve and seek support from others."

Fear:
Message: "There may be a threat or danger. Assess the situation and take appropriate precautions."

Anxiety:
Message: "You may be facing uncertainty or potential danger. It's important to plan and prepare, but excessive worry can be counterproductive."

Guilt:
Message: "You believe you have done something that goes against your values or harmed someone. Use this feeling as a signal to make amends or change your behavior."

Shame:
Message: "You feel unworthy or flawed, but remember that everyone makes mistakes. Use this as motivation for personal growth and self-compassion."

Jealousy:
Message: "You feel threatened by a perceived loss or threat to a relationship or possession. Use this feeling as an opportunity to communicate openly and address insecurities."

Envy:
Message: "You desire something someone else has. Instead of resenting them, use this feeling as motivation to set goals and work towards what you want."

Frustration:
Message: "You are facing obstacles or barriers. See this as a challenge to problem-solve and persevere."

Regret:
Message: "You wish you had made a different choice in the past. Learn from your regrets and make more informed decisions in the future."

Loneliness:
Message: "You may be lacking social connection or meaningful relationships. Use this as a cue to seek out opportunities for connection."

Disgust:
Message: "You are encountering something that goes against your sense of cleanliness or morality. This feeling can help you avoid potentially harmful situations."

Despair:
Message: "You may feel overwhelmed by hopelessness or helplessness. Reach out for support and consider seeking professional help."

Bitterness:
Message: "You feel resentment or anger over past injustices or grievances. Recognize the need to process these feelings and, if possible, seek resolution or closure."

Hurt:
Message: "You have been emotionally wounded by someone's actions or words. Communicate your feelings and seek understanding or reconciliation."

It's important to remember that negative emotions are not inherently "bad" but are natural responses to life's challenges. They can provide valuable insights and motivation for growth, change, and self-care. Acknowledging and understanding these emotions can help individuals navigate their experiences and make informed decisions to improve their overall well-being.

UNDERSTANDING
DEPRESSION
ANXIETY
TRAUMA
& COPING SKILLS

Depression Symptoms

@DrJadaJackson

Depression is a common but serious mental health disorder that affects how a person feels, thinks, and handles daily activities.

Persistent sadness

"I feel sad all the time, even when nothing bad is happening."

Hopelessness

"I feel like things will never get better, no matter what I do."

Loss of interest

"I feel like I don't care about the things I used to enjoy anymore."

Worthlessness

"I feel like I'm not good enough and that I can't do anything right."

Irritability

"I feel irritated by everything, even small things that shouldn't bother me."

Thoughts of death or suicide

"I feel like everyone would be better off without me, and sometimes I think about ending it."

Fatigue

"I feel exhausted all the time, even when I haven't done anything."

Sleep disturbances

"I feel like I can't sleep, or I sleep too much but never feel rested."

Changes in appetite

"I feel like I either have no appetite or I can't stop eating, even when I'm not hungry."

Social withdrawal

"I feel like isolating myself from everyone because I don't have the energy to be around people."

Decreased motivation

"I feel like I have no motivation to start or finish anything, even simple tasks."

Increased use of alcohol or drugs

"I feel like I'm drinking or using substances more to escape from how I'm feeling."

Anxiety Symptoms

@DrJadaJackson

Anxiety symptoms are the physical, emotional, and behavioral reactions that occur when a person feels anxious or stressed.

Rapid Heartbeat

"I feel like my heart is racing, and it makes me anxious that something might be wrong with me."

Shortness of breath

"I feel like I can't catch my breath, and it makes me panic, like I'm suffocating."

Sweating

"I feel like I'm sweating more than usual, and it's making me uncomfortable and self-conscious."

Trembling

"I feel like my hands are shaking, and it makes me feel out of control."

Muscle tension

"I feel tightness in my neck and shoulders, and it's making me physically exhausted."

Irritability

"I feel tightness in my neck and shoulders, and it's making me physically exhausted."

Headaches

"I feel like I have a constant headache, and it's hard to focus on anything else."

Upset stomach

"I feel nauseous and my stomach hurts, especially when I get anxious."

Fatigue

"I feel drained and tired all the time, even when I haven't done much."

Excessive worry

"I feel like I can't stop worrying about things that may never happen."

Racing thoughts

"I feel like my thoughts are racing, and I can't slow them down no matter how hard I try."

Sleep disturbances

"I feel like I can't fall asleep or stay asleep because my mind won't stop worrying."

Understanding Everyday Trauma

Here are types of everyday trauma that can impact emotional
and mental well-being

Workplace Trauma

"I feel powerless and belittled when I'm constantly criticized or bullied at work."

Relationship Trauma

"I feel worthless when I'm constantly criticized and never feel good enough."

Financial Trauma

"I feel ashamed and stressed, constantly worrying about how to pay bills and make ends meet."

Parenting Trauma

"I feel exhausted and overwhelmed trying to care for my children without enough support."

Social Trauma

"I feel lonely and excluded, like no one truly understands or accepts me."

Health-Related Trauma

"I feel drained and scared because my illness never seems to improve."

Cultural/Societal Trauma

"I feel hurt and angry when I'm treated differently because of my identity."

Housing Insecurity

"I feel vulnerable and uncertain about where I will live next or if I'll have a home at all."

Academic Trauma

"I feel constant pressure to succeed academically, and it's draining my energy and confidence."

Digital Trauma

"I feel attacked and powerless when I experience cyberbullying or online harassment."

Caregiver Trauma

"I feel exhausted and emotionally drained from constantly caring for my loved one with no break."

Food Insecurity

"I feel anxious every day not knowing if I'll have enough food for myself or my family."

@DrJadaJackson

Everyday Coping Skills

@DrJadaJackson

Emotional Coping Skills

1. Deep Breathing – Practice slow, deep breaths to calm the nervous system.
2. Progressive Muscle Relaxation – Tense and relax muscle groups to reduce physical tension.
3. Journaling – Write down thoughts, feelings, or events to process emotions.
4. Visualization – Picture a peaceful or happy place to reduce anxiety or stress.
5. Affirmations – Use positive self-talk to reframe negative thoughts.
6. Cry it Out – Allow yourself to cry as a way to release built-up emotions.
7. Practice Gratitude – Focus on the things you are thankful for to shift your mindset.

Physical Coping Skills

1. Exercise – Engage in physical activity, like walking, running, or yoga, to boost mood.
2. Stretching – Gentle stretching to relieve tension and improve body awareness.
3. Dancing – Move freely to your favorite music to release pent-up energy.
4. Engage in a Hobby – Do something you enjoy, like gardening, knitting, or painting.

Social Coping Skills

1. Talk to a Trusted Friend or Family Member – Share what's on your mind with someone you trust.
2. Join a Support Group – Connect with others who share similar experiences.
3. Volunteer – Helping others can provide perspective and lift your mood.
4. Set Boundaries – Learn to say no and create personal space when needed.
5. Seek Professional Help – Schedule regular therapy sessions or check-ins.

Cognitive Coping Skills

1. Thought Stopping – Interrupt negative thoughts by saying "stop" out loud or in your head.
2. Reframing – Challenge and change negative or distorted thoughts.
3. Problem Solving – Break down problems into manageable steps and brainstorm solutions.
4. Mind Mapping – Organize your thoughts visually on paper to gain perspective.
5. Focus on What You Can Control – Make a list of controllable aspects to reduce overwhelm.

The STOP METHOD

The STOP Method is a mindfulness-based technique used for emotional regulation, helping individuals pause and manage their emotions before reacting impulsively. Each step encourages greater awareness and control over emotional responses.

S

STOP
- **Description:** The first step is to literally stop what you're doing when you notice a strong emotional reaction. This pause interrupts the automatic response, preventing immediate, often impulsive, reactions. It allows space for you to become aware of your emotions and their intensity before acting.
- **Purpose:** Create a moment of interruption to avoid reactive behavior.

T

TAKE A BREATH
- **Description:** After stopping, take a slow, deep breath. This simple act helps calm the nervous system, grounding you in the present moment. Deep breathing reduces the physiological effects of stress, like a racing heart or shallow breathing, and brings clarity to your thoughts.
- **Purpose:** Lower stress and gain mental clarity by focusing on the breath.

O

OBSERVE
- **Description:** Observe what is happening internally and externally. Ask yourself what you're feeling emotionally and physically. Notice your thoughts, body sensations (e.g., tension, tightness), and the situation you're in. This helps build awareness of your emotional state without judgment.
- **Purpose:** Increase self-awareness by noticing your thoughts, feelings, and environment.

P

PROCEED
- **Description:** After you've paused, breathed, and observed, proceed mindfully with a thoughtful response. Rather than reacting impulsively, choose a response that aligns with your values and goals, whether that means communicating calmly, setting boundaries, or simply walking away.
- **Purpose:** Act with intention rather than reacting on impulse, leading to better emotional regulation and decision-making.

The STOP Method helps slow down emotional reactions, allowing for better emotional control and mindful responses in challenging situations.

@DrJadaJackson

UNDERSTAND YOUR PERSONALITY

Find Your Personality Type: Accessible Ways to Take the Myers-Briggs Test

Taking the Myers-Briggs Personality Assessment can be an insightful way for you to better understand your unique personality traits and how they influence your daily life, decision-making, and interactions with others. There are several ways you can take this assessment. You can access free versions online, although these may not always provide the depth and accuracy of the official test. The most accurate and comprehensive option is through the official Myers-Briggs Type Indicator (MBTI) website, which offers a more detailed report and analysis of your results. Additionally, many certified MBTI practitioners, including mental health professionals, offer the test as part of coaching or counseling services, allowing for personalized feedback and guidance based on your results. Whether you prefer a quick online version or a more thorough, guided experience, taking the MBTI assessment can give you valuable insights into your strengths, communication style, and work preferences, helping you navigate relationships and career choices more effectively.

- Official MBTI Website: The most accurate and comprehensive option is taking the official Myers-Briggs Type Indicator (MBTI) assessment through the MBTI website. This version includes an in-depth report and professional insights into your personality type.
- Free Online Versions: Various websites offer free versions of the Myers-Briggs assessment, such as 16Personalities and Truity. While not as detailed as the official test, these versions can still give you a quick overview of your personality type.
- Certified MBTI Practitioner: You can work with a certified MBTI practitioner or licensed counselor who offers the test. This option provides personalized feedback and a more professional interpretation of your results in a coaching or therapeutic setting.

Understanding who you are is a crucial step toward personal growth and mental well-being. By gaining insight into your personality, such as through the Myers-Briggs assessment, you can begin to understand why you approach challenges the way you do, how you make decisions, and why you connect with others in certain ways.

Psychologically, self-awareness leads to improved emotional regulation, stronger interpersonal relationships, and better stress management. When you understand your personality, you're empowered to embrace your strengths and work on areas of improvement. This knowledge also fosters self-compassion, helping you to make more aligned decisions in both your personal and professional life. In essence, learning about who you are sets the foundation for living a more balanced, authentic, and fulfilling life.

16 Personalities.com

Myers-Briggs Type Indicator (MBTI) Breakdown

In the Myers-Briggs Type Indicator (MBTI), each personality type is represented by four letters, where each letter stands for a specific preference in how a person interacts with the world, makes decisions, and processes information. Here's a breakdown of what each letter represents:

Introversion (I) vs. Extroversion (E)

1. Introversion (I) vs. Extroversion (E)

This dimension represents where people focus their attention and get their energy from:

- **Introversion (I):**
  - Focus on internal thoughts, feelings, and reflections.
  - Energized by time alone.
  - Tend to process ideas internally before sharing.
  - Prefer deep, meaningful interactions over large social gatherings.
- **Extroversion (E):**
  - Focus on the external world, people, and activities.
  - Energized by interacting with others.
  - Think out loud and tend to share ideas as they form.
  - Enjoy being the center of attention and prefer engaging in group settings.

Sensing (S) vs. Intuition (N)

2. Sensing (S) vs. Intuition (N)

This dimension represents how people prefer to take in information:

- **Sensing (S):**
  - Focus on facts, details, and the present moment.
  - Prefer concrete, practical information.
  - Tend to trust experiences and observations.
  - Like step-by-step processes and are detail-oriented.
- **Intuition (N):**
  - Focus on patterns, possibilities, and the future.
  - Prefer abstract, theoretical information.
  - Enjoy imagining possibilities and exploring big ideas.
  - Tend to think about the long-term implications of actions.

Thinking (T) vs. Feeling (F)

3. Thinking (T) vs. Feeling (F)
This dimension reflects how people prefer to make decisions:
- **Thinking (T):**
  - Make decisions based on logic and objective criteria.
  - Value fairness and consistency.
  - Tend to be more critical and direct in communication.
  - Focus on tasks, data, and facts rather than emotions.
- **Feeling (F):**
  - Make decisions based on personal values and how decisions affect others.
  - Value harmony, empathy, and cooperation.
  - Tend to be more considerate and tactful in communication.
  - Focus on relationships and people's emotions in decision-making.

Judging (J) vs. Perceiving (P)

4. Judging (J) vs. Perceiving (P)
This dimension reflects how people prefer to structure their lives:
- **Judging (J):**
  - Prefer structure, order, and predictability.
  - Like to plan ahead and stick to schedules.
  - Enjoy having decisions made and tasks completed.
  - Prefer clear rules and guidelines in their work and personal life.
- **Perceiving (P):**
  - Prefer flexibility, spontaneity, and openness.
  - Like to keep options open and adapt to new information.
  - Tend to work in bursts of energy, often waiting until the last minute to complete tasks.
  - Enjoy exploring possibilities rather than settling on a decision too quickly.

Summary of the Four Dimensions:
- **I vs. E:** How you gain energy (internal vs. external world)
- **S vs. N:** How you gather information (facts vs. possibilities)
- **T vs. F:** How you make decisions (logic vs. values)
- **J vs. P:** How you approach life (structure vs. flexibility)

These combinations create the 16 unique personality types in the Myers-Briggs framework. Understanding these letters and dimensions can help improve interpersonal relationships, especially in the workplace, by recognizing and valuing different communication and decision-making styles. @DrJadaJackson

What You Need to Know About Personalities

@JadaJackson

Personality Name	Strengths	Weaknesses	Workplace Function	Compatible Personalities	Tips for Working Together
Architect (INTJ)	Strategic, decisive, independent	Dismissive of emotions, arrogant	Planners and problem solvers, ex: designing long-term strategies	ENTJ, ENTP, INFJ	Value their independence but keep communication clear and logical
Logician (INTP)	Analytical, open-minded, creative	Perfectionistic, forgetful of details	Innovators and critical thinkers, ex: solving complex technical problems	INTJ, ENTP, INFP	Give them space to explore ideas, and encourage structured deadlines
Commander (ENTJ)	Efficient, strategic, confident	Stubborn, impatient	Natural leaders, ex: managing a project team towards a clear goal	INTJ, ENTP, ESTJ	Focus on shared goals and avoid personal conflicts
Debater (ENTP)	Quick-witted, enthusiastic, charismatic	Argumentative, insensitive	Idea generators and challengers, ex: brainstorming new business concepts	INTJ, ENTJ, INTP	Encourage constructive debate but ensure mutual respect
Advocate (INFJ)	Insightful, altruistic, decisive	Sensitive, perfectionistic	Idealistic leaders, ex: developing people-focused policies	INFP, ENFJ, INTJ	Foster a mission-driven environment to align on shared values
Mediator (INFP)	Empathetic, open-minded, creative	Overly idealistic, impractical	Creative problem solvers, ex: developing meaningful content	INFJ, ENFP, ENFJ	Encourage them to express ideas freely but manage deadlines gently
Protagonist (ENFJ)	Charismatic, inspiring, natural leaders	Overly sensitive, selfless to a fault	Motivational leaders, ex: leading a team with emotional intelligence	INFJ, ENFP, ESFJ	Acknowledge their contributions and keep open communication
Campaigner (ENFP)	Curious, enthusiastic, social	Easily stressed, overthinks	Team motivators and idea generators, ex: initiating creative projects	INFP, ENFJ, INFJ	Encourage free-flowing ideas, but help them prioritize goals

What You Need to Know About Personalities @JadaJackson

Personality Name	Strengths	Weaknesses	Workplace Function	Compatible Personalities	Tips for Working Together
Logistician (ISTJ)	Organized, responsible, meticulous	Stubborn, resistant to change	Responsible task managers, ex: handling detailed project logistics	ESTJ, ISTP, ISFJ	Communicate clearly and provide structured environments
Defender (ISFJ)	Supportive, reliable, meticulous	Reluctant to change, overly modest	Detail-oriented and reliable, ex: ensuring consistent customer service	ESTJ, ESFJ, ISTJ	Value their support and provide clear instructions
Executive (ESTJ)	Organized, dependable, leadership-oriented	Inflexible, critical	Efficient organizers, ex: managing teams for optimal efficiency	ISTJ, ESFJ, ISFJ	Set clear objectives and respect their need for order
Consul (ESFJ)	Supportive, outgoing, practical	Overly selfless, sensitive to criticism	Team-focused collaborators, ex: managing group dynamics in service industries	ISFJ, ESFP, ENFJ	Show appreciation for their support and avoid unnecessary criticism
Virtuoso (ISTP)	Bold, practical, creative problem-solvers	Impulsive, easily bored	Hands-on workers, ex: tackling immediate technical challenges	ESTP, INTP, ISTJ	Give them space to work independently but set deadlines
Adventurer (ISFP)	Artistic, flexible, curious	Unpredictable, easily stressed	Creative and adaptable, ex: developing artistic projects	ESFP, INFP, ENFP	Appreciate their creativity, but guide them with clear goals
Entrepreneur (ESTP)	Energetic, practical, bold	Impulsive, risk-prone	Action-oriented and quick decision-makers, ex: handling crisis management	ISTP, ESFP, ENTP	Focus on tangible outcomes and align on shared risks
Entertainer (ESFP)	Outgoing, creative, spontaneous	Unfocused, easily bored	Social, team-builders, ex: managing public-facing or social roles	ISFP, ESFJ, ENFP	Encourage creativity while keeping them focused on task priorities

16 PERSONALITIES.COM

Personality Types That Work Well Together:

- INTJ: ENTJ, INTP, ENFP
- ENTP: INTJ, INTP, ENFP
- INFJ: ENFJ, INFP, INTJ
- ISFJ: ESFJ, ESTJ, ISTJ
- ENTJ: INTJ, INTP, ESTJ
- INFP: INFJ, ENFJ, ENFP
- ESFJ: ISFJ, ESTJ, ENFJ
- ISTJ: ESTJ, ISFJ, ISTP
- ENFJ: INFJ, INFP, ESFJ
- ESFP: ISFP, ENFP, ESFJ
- ESTP: ISTP, ESTJ, ESFP

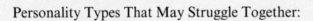

Personality Types That May Struggle Together:

- INTJ & ESFP: Logical vs. emotional conflict
- ISTJ & ENFP: Structured vs. flexible approaches
- ENTP & ISFJ: Innovation vs. tradition clash
- ISFP & ESTJ: Free-spirited vs. rule-oriented
- INFP & ENTJ: Sensitivity vs. command style conflict

Understanding and embracing different personality types in the workplace is essential for building strong teams that leverage the strengths of each member. Even when personalities clash, mutual respect and adaptive strategies can create an environment where differing perspectives lead to more robust outcomes.

By fostering open communication, encouraging empathy, and finding middle ground between differing approaches, teams can thrive even when their members come from diverse personality backgrounds.

Leadership Based on Personality Types Worksheet

Instructions:

Use this worksheet to identify the personality types in your team and apply specific strategies to lead them effectively. Fill in each section based on your team members' strengths, communication preferences, and how they approach tasks.

1. Identify Team Members' Personality Types

- List out the team members and their Myers-Briggs personality types (if known). If unsure, use the brief descriptions of each type to estimate.
- Note: If personality types are not formally assessed, use this as a reference guide to observe tendencies.

Team Member	Personality Type	Key Strengths	Areas for Development
Example: John	ENTJ	Leadership, strategic thinking	Patience, flexibility

2. Assign Roles Based on Strengths

Leaders should align tasks with individual strengths rather than expecting everyone to operate the same way. Use the table below to assign roles that fit each personality type's preferences.

- Judging (J) types tend to prefer structured, leadership roles.
- Perceiving (P) types may prefer flexible, creative tasks.
- Thinking (T) types work well with data and analysis.
- Feeling (F) types excel in people-focused or collaborative roles.

Team Member	Strength	Suggested Role	Task Example
Example: John	Decision-making, strategy	Project lead	Leading the development of a new product
Example: Jane	Empathy, creativity	Team morale support	Organizing team-building events

3. Create Shared Goals

Often, conflict arises from different priorities among team members. Use this section to define shared goals that all personality types can align with, even if they approach them differently.

Goal	Why It Matters to the Team	How Each Personality Type Can Contribute
Example: Increase customer satisfaction by 15%	It benefits both company success and client happiness	ENTJ: Lead strategy implementation INFP: Focus on improving customer empathy ISTJ: Manage operational details

Key Considerations:

Introverted (I) types may prefer working independently toward shared goals.

Extroverted (E) types may prefer collaborative team efforts.

Ensure both get space to contribute according to their preferences.

@DrJadaJackson

Leadership Based on Personality Types Worksheet cont.

4. Encourage Open Communication

Effective communication varies depending on personality type. Use this section to plan communication strategies that fit your team's needs.

Personality Type	Preferred Communication Style	Action Plan
Example: INTP	Needs clarity, prefers written communication	Provide detailed project guidelines in writing, follow up with in-person Q&A
Example: ENFP	Enjoys brainstorming verbally	Host regular brainstorming sessions to encourage creative input

Tips for Communication:

Thinking (T) types prefer logical, data-driven discussions.

Feeling (F) types appreciate emotionally sensitive, collaborative approaches.

Balance direct feedback with positive reinforcement.

5. Resolve Conflicts and Enhance Collaboration

Conflicts between differing personality types can arise due to opposing preferences. Identify potential clashes and create strategies for resolution and collaboration.

Potential Clash	Personality Types Involved	Resolution Strategy
Example: Structure vs. Flexibility	ISTJ vs. ENFP	Set a clear deadline (ISTJ need) but allow flexibility in how tasks are completed (ENFP need)
Introversion vs. Extroversion	INTJ vs. ESFJ	Allow INTJ solo work time, schedule collaborative tasks when they feel ready to contribute

6. Leadership Action Plan

Based on your team's personality types and needs, create a leadership action plan for implementing the strategies outlined in this worksheet.

Step 1: Identify key strengths and roles for each team member.

Step 2: Set shared goals that allow different approaches.

Step 3: Establish clear, open communication practices based on team preferences.

Step 4: Proactively resolve potential conflicts by understanding personality-based clashes.

Step 5: Regularly review team dynamics and adjust strategies as needed.

Action Plan Example:

Assign John (ENTJ) to lead project execution.

Schedule bi-weekly brainstorming sessions for Jane (ENFP) to express creative ideas.

Set shared project milestones that balance structure and flexibility.

Provide written guidelines for tasks to accommodate introverted team members like Alice (INTJ).

Organize a team-building event to foster better understanding between conflicting types.

@DrJadaJackson

7. Reflection and Review

After implementing the strategies, review team performance and note areas for improvement.

What Worked Well	Areas for Improvement	Action Plan
Example: Open communication improved	Conflict between ISTJ and ENFP on task timelines	Create a more flexible deadline process that accounts for personality needs

Conclusion:

By understanding and utilizing personality types in the workplace, leaders can optimize team performance, enhance communication, and reduce conflict. Use this worksheet as an ongoing tool to refine leadership strategies and ensure every team member thrives in their role.

The High 5 Test

High5Test.com

The High 5 Test is a strengths-based assessment designed to help individuals, teams, and organizations identify their top five strengths. It focuses on unlocking a person's full potential by recognizing what energizes and motivates them. The goal is to leverage these strengths in everyday life, including in leadership and teamwork, allowing individuals and teams to be more productive, engaged, and fulfilled.

Leadership Worksheet: Leveraging High 5 Strengths

Worksheet Objective:

This worksheet is designed to help leaders understand their strengths through the High 5 Test and apply these strengths to their leadership role. It encourages self-reflection, goal setting, and practical steps for leveraging strengths in real-world leadership situations.

Part 1: Identify Your High 5 Strengths

- List your High 5 strengths below (from the test results):
  - Strength 1: _____
  - Strength 2: _____
  - Strength 3: _____
  - Strength 4: _____
  - Strength 5: _____
- Reflect on your strengths:
  - Which strength do you use most often in your leadership role?
  - Which strength surprises you, or do you think you don't use enough?

Part 2: Strengths in Action

1. Strengths at Work: Reflect on a recent leadership experience or challenge. How did you use your strengths to address it?
   - Example/situation: _____
   - Strength used: _____
   - Outcome: _____
2. Potential Areas for Improvement: Identify an area in your leadership role where you feel challenged. How could your strengths help you in this area?
   - Challenge: _____
   - Strength to apply: _____
   - Action plan: _____

@DrJadaJackson

The High 5 Test

High5Test.com

Part 3: Applying Strengths to Team Development

Recognizing Strengths in Your Team:

As a leader, why is it important to recognize the strengths of your team members?

How can you leverage the strengths of your team to improve collaboration and performance?

Practical Steps for Strengths-based Leadership:

Delegate tasks based on team members' strengths. Identify an example where you can apply this principle in your leadership role.

Foster a culture of strengths recognition: What will you do to ensure your team members know their strengths and can use them?

Part 4: Action Plan for Leadership Growth

1. Goal Setting: Based on your High 5 strengths, write down 3 goals for your leadership development over the next 6 months.
   - Goal 1: _____
   - Goal 2: _____
   - Goal 3: _____
2. Accountability: How will you hold yourself accountable for applying your strengths to these goals? Who will support you in this process?

Part 5: Reflection and Growth

1. End-of-Month Reflection: At the end of each month, reflect on how you've applied your strengths to your leadership. What worked well, and what could you improve?
   - What progress did you make toward your leadership goals?
   - Which strengths were most helpful in achieving your goals?
   - What will you do differently next month?

This worksheet helps leaders understand and maximize their strengths to become more effective and engaged in their roles. The process of reflection, goal setting, and practical application ensures that strengths are not only identified but actively used in leadership development.

@DrJadaJackson

Attachment Styles Worksheet

Introduction

Attachment theory explains how early relationships with caregivers influence how we connect with others in adulthood. There are four primary attachment styles: Secure, Anxious, Avoidant, and Disorganized. Each one impacts how we interact in close relationships, from friendships to romantic partnerships.

Part 1: Identifying Your Attachment Style

Below are descriptions of the four main attachment styles. Read through them carefully and reflect on which one resonates with you the most.

1. Secure Attachment

- Characteristics: You feel comfortable with closeness and intimacy, trust others, and have a balanced sense of independence.
- In Relationships: You communicate openly, feel comfortable relying on others, and can resolve conflicts in a healthy way.
- Reflection:
  - Do you feel comfortable trusting others and depending on them?
  - Are you able to express your emotions and needs openly?

2. Anxious Attachment

- Characteristics: You may fear abandonment, crave closeness, and seek constant reassurance.
- In Relationships: You often feel insecure or overly dependent on your partner, may experience jealousy, and worry about being unworthy of love.
- Reflection:
  - Do you often feel anxious or afraid your partner might leave you?
  - Do you need frequent reassurance that your partner loves and values you?

3. Avoidant Attachment

- Characteristics: You tend to avoid intimacy, value independence, and may feel uncomfortable with closeness.
- In Relationships: You may struggle to open up emotionally, keep your partner at a distance, or prioritize personal space over emotional connection.
- Reflection:
  - Do you find it difficult to rely on others or allow them to get too close?
  - Do you prefer to handle problems on your own rather than ask for help?

4. Disorganized (Fearful-Avoidant) Attachment

- Characteristics: You may experience a mix of anxiety and avoidance, often feeling confused about relationships.
- In Relationships: You may fear intimacy and closeness while also craving connection, leading to unpredictable or inconsistent behavior.
- Reflection:
  - Do you feel conflicted about relationships, wanting closeness but also fearing it?
  - Do you find yourself pushing people away even when you want them to stay?

Attachment Styles Worksheet

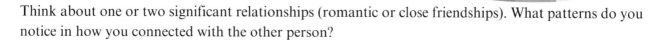

Part 2: Exploring Your Relationship Patterns

Describe Your Past Relationships:

Think about one or two significant relationships (romantic or close friendships). What patterns do you notice in how you connected with the other person?

Relationship 1:_____

Relationship 2:_____

Triggers and Reactions:

- What situations in relationships tend to make you feel insecure, anxious, or withdrawn?
- How do you typically react when you feel these emotions?

Attachment in Childhood
- Reflect on your early childhood relationships with your caregivers. Do any memories stand out about how they responded to your needs for comfort or independence?

Attachment in Current Relationships
- How does your attachment style show up in your current relationships (romantic, friendships, family)?
- Are there any specific behaviors you'd like to change?

Part 3: Reframing Your Attachment Style

- Self-Compassion: Understand that attachment styles are not "bad" or "good"—they're coping mechanisms you developed based on your experiences. How can you show yourself compassion for the patterns you've developed?

   _____

- Growth in Relationships:
   What changes would you like to make in your approach to relationships?

   _____

   What strategies can help you develop healthier attachment behaviors? (e.g., open communication, seeking reassurance, setting boundaries)

   _____

- Actions for Secure Attachment:
   List 2-3 actions you can take to move toward a more secure attachment style. 1. 2. 3.

   _____

DEVELOP
THE GROWTH
MINDSET

FIVE

THINGS YOU SHOULD KNOW

GROWTH MINDSET

1 DEFINITION

A growth mindset is the belief that abilities and intelligence can be developed through effort, learning, and perseverance.

2 WHY IT'S IMPORTANT

- Encourages resilience.
- Promotes continuous learning.
- Increases motivation.
- Builds confidence.
- Leads to higher achievement.

3 EXAMPLES

- Learning from mistakes and improving.
- Taking on challenges to grow.
- Using feedback for self-improvement.

4 REFLECTION QUESTIONS

- How do you usually respond to challenges?
- Where can you apply more effort to improve?
- What's one thing you can tell yourself to stay motivated during tough times?

5 ACTION STEPS

- Replace negative self-talk with positive affirmations.
- Focus on learning, not just outcomes.
- Embrace effort and persistence.
- Seek and use feedback constructively.

six
effective ways to develop a
Growth Mindset

1 **Embrace Challenges**

View challenges as opportunities to learn and grow, rather than something to avoid. They offer valuable experiences that can enhance your skills and understanding. Embracing challenges helps you become more adaptable and resilient in the face of difficulties.

2

Learn from Mistakes

Accept failure as part of the learning process, recognizing that each setback is a stepping stone to success. Analyze mistakes to understand what went wrong, adjust your approach, and use them as valuable lessons for future growth.

3

Replace Negative Self-Talk

Swap "I can't" with "I'm learning how to." Focus on progress rather than perfection.

4

Celebrate Effort, Not Just Results

Acknowledge the hard work you put in, even if the outcome isn't perfect, and recognize that consistent effort leads to gradual improvement. Effort is key to growth.

6

Surround Yourself with Growth- Oriented People

Engage with people who inspire you to keep learning and improving. Their mindset can positively influence yours.

5 **Seek Feedback**

Use feedback as a tool for improvement, not as criticism, and approach it with an open mind to gain new insights. It can help you identify areas where you can grow and refine your skills to achieve better results.

@DrJadaJackson

UNDERSTAND
DYSFUNCTIONAL
FAMILY ROLES

Eleven

Commom Dysfunctional family Roles

1 The Hero

The Hero, often the eldest child, takes on adult responsibilities early and strives to present the family as functional through overachievement in academics or other areas. They compensate for family problems by appearing highly competent but may struggle with anxiety, stress, and perfectionism. This role often leads them to suppress their own needs and emotions in an effort to maintain the facade of normalcy.

2 The Scapegoat

The Scapegoat is the family member blamed for the family's problems and often acts out or rebels to deflect attention from the dysfunction. This role leads to feelings of rejection, anger, and low self-esteem, which may manifest in defiant or self-destructive behaviors.

3 The Mascot

The Mascot uses humor to deflect attention from the family's issues, often acting as the entertainer to lighten the mood. They seek approval through jokes and try to keep everyone happy. However, this role leads to struggles with intimacy and authenticity, as they use humor to mask deeper feelings of anxiety or sadness.

4 The Lost Child

The Lost Child withdraws from family dysfunction by becoming quiet, isolated, and emotionally detached, often spending time alone to avoid conflict. This role leads to feelings of neglect, social anxiety, and difficulty forming close relationships.

5 The Caretaker (or Enabler)

The Caretaker enables the dysfunctional behavior by taking on emotional and physical responsibilities, often making excuses or covering for the problematic family member. This leads to feelings of exhaustion, poor boundaries, and neglect of their own needs.

6 The Manipulator

The Manipulator controls family dynamics through lies and emotional blackmail, often playing members against each other to maintain power. Their insecurity leads to trust issues and anxiety about losing control.

@DrJadaJackson

Eleven

Commom
Dysfunctional
family
Roles

⑦ The Addict or Troubled One

The Addict or Troubled One struggles with addiction or mental health issues, often engaging in destructive behaviors and hiding their problems from others. They experience deep shame, guilt, and denial, which leads to difficulties with accountability, self-esteem, and maintaining healthy relationships.

⑧ The Persecutor

The Persecutor uses aggression, whether verbal, emotional, or physical, to dominate and control other family members, maintaining authority through fear and intimidation. Beneath their aggression, they often feel powerless and insecure, masking unresolved anger and deep-seated fear.

⑨ The Fixer

The Fixer feels responsible for solving everyone else's problems, constantly offering advice, intervening in conflicts, and neglecting their own needs. This leads to feelings of being overburdened, frustrated, and unappreciated, often at the cost of their personal growth and self-care.

⑩ The Victim

The Victim portrays themselves as helpless and powerless, often avoiding accountability for their role in the family's dysfunction. They manipulate others with self-pity, leading to feelings of being stuck, disempowered, and overwhelmed by chronic negative emotions.

⑪ The Golden Child

The Golden Child is favored by one or both parents, receiving preferential treatment that often leads to resentment and division within the family. While they may feel pressure to meet high expectations, this role can result in arrogance, entitlement, or guilt over the favoritism they experience.

@DrJadaJackson

Made in the USA
Columbia, SC
23 October 2024

44968407R00031